The INTJ Female

How to Understand and Embrace Your Unique MBTI Personality as an INTJ Woman

HowExpert with Caitlin Humbert

Copyright HowExpert™
www.HowExpert.com

For more tips related to this topic, visit HowExpert.com/intjfemale.

Recommended Resources

- HowExpert.com – Quick 'How To' Guides on All Topics from A to Z by Everyday Experts.
- HowExpert.com/free – Free HowExpert Email Newsletter.
- HowExpert.com/books – HowExpert Books
- HowExpert.com/courses – HowExpert Courses
- HowExpert.com/clothing – HowExpert Clothing
- HowExpert.com/membership – HowExpert Membership Site
- HowExpert.com/affiliates – HowExpert Affiliate Program
- HowExpert.com/writers – Write About Your #1 Passion/Knowledge/Expertise & Become a HowExpert Author.
- HowExpert.com/resources – Additional HowExpert Recommended Resources
- YouTube.com/HowExpert – Subscribe to HowExpert YouTube.
- Instagram.com/HowExpert – Follow HowExpert on Instagram.
- Facebook.com/HowExpert – Follow HowExpert on Facebook.

COPYRIGHT, LEGAL NOTICE AND DISCLAIMER:

COPYRIGHT © BY HOWEXPERT™ (OWNED BY HOT METHODS). ALL RIGHTS RESERVED WORLDWIDE. NO PART OF THIS PUBLICATION MAY BE REPRODUCED IN ANY FORM OR BY ANY MEANS, INCLUDING SCANNING, PHOTOCOPYING, OR OTHERWISE WITHOUT PRIOR WRITTEN PERMISSION OF THE COPYRIGHT HOLDER.

DISCLAIMER AND TERMS OF USE: PLEASE NOTE THAT MUCH OF THIS PUBLICATION IS BASED ON PERSONAL EXPERIENCE AND ANECDOTAL EVIDENCE. ALTHOUGH THE AUTHOR AND PUBLISHER HAVE MADE EVERY REASONABLE ATTEMPT TO ACHIEVE COMPLETE ACCURACY OF THE CONTENT IN THIS GUIDE, THEY ASSUME NO RESPONSIBILITY FOR ERRORS OR OMISSIONS. ALSO, YOU SHOULD USE THIS INFORMATION AS YOU SEE FIT, AND AT YOUR OWN RISK. YOUR PARTICULAR SITUATION MAY NOT BE EXACTLY SUITED TO THE EXAMPLES ILLUSTRATED HERE; IN FACT, IT'S LIKELY THAT THEY WON'T BE THE SAME, AND YOU SHOULD ADJUST YOUR USE OF THE INFORMATION AND RECOMMENDATIONS ACCORDINGLY.

THE AUTHOR AND PUBLISHER DO NOT WARRANT THE PERFORMANCE, EFFECTIVENESS OR APPLICABILITY OF ANY SITES LISTED OR LINKED TO IN THIS BOOK. ALL LINKS ARE FOR INFORMATION PURPOSES ONLY AND ARE NOT WARRANTED FOR CONTENT, ACCURACY OR ANY OTHER IMPLIED OR EXPLICIT PURPOSE.

ANY TRADEMARKS, SERVICE MARKS, PRODUCT NAMES OR NAMED FEATURES ARE ASSUMED TO BE THE PROPERTY OF THEIR RESPECTIVE OWNERS, AND ARE USED ONLY FOR REFERENCE. THERE IS NO IMPLIED ENDORSEMENT IF WE USE ONE OF THESE TERMS.

NO PART OF THIS BOOK MAY BE REPRODUCED, STORED IN A RETRIEVAL SYSTEM, OR TRANSMITTED BY ANY OTHER MEANS: ELECTRONIC, MECHANICAL, PHOTOCOPYING, RECORDING, OR OTHERWISE, WITHOUT THE PRIOR WRITTEN PERMISSION OF THE AUTHOR.

ANY VIOLATION BY STEALING THIS BOOK OR DOWNLOADING OR SHARING IT ILLEGALLY WILL BE PROSECUTED BY LAWYERS TO THE FULLEST EXTENT. THIS PUBLICATION IS PROTECTED UNDER THE US COPYRIGHT ACT OF 1976 AND ALL OTHER APPLICABLE INTERNATIONAL, FEDERAL, STATE AND LOCAL LAWS AND ALL RIGHTS ARE RESERVED, INCLUDING RESALE RIGHTS: YOU ARE NOT ALLOWED TO GIVE OR SELL THIS GUIDE TO ANYONE ELSE.

THIS PUBLICATION IS DESIGNED TO PROVIDE ACCURATE AND AUTHORITATIVE INFORMATION WITH REGARD TO THE SUBJECT MATTER COVERED. IT IS SOLD WITH THE UNDERSTANDING THAT THE AUTHORS AND PUBLISHERS ARE NOT ENGAGED IN RENDERING LEGAL, FINANCIAL, OR OTHER PROFESSIONAL ADVICE. LAWS AND PRACTICES OFTEN VARY FROM STATE TO STATE AND IF LEGAL OR OTHER EXPERT ASSISTANCE IS REQUIRED, THE SERVICES OF A PROFESSIONAL SHOULD BE SOUGHT. THE AUTHORS AND PUBLISHER SPECIFICALLY DISCLAIM ANY LIABILITY THAT IS INCURRED FROM THE USE OR APPLICATION OF THE CONTENTS OF THIS BOOK.

COPYRIGHT BY HOWEXPERT™ (OWNED BY HOT METHODS)
ALL RIGHTS RESERVED WORLDWIDE.

Table of Contents

Recommended Resources 2
Chapter 1: What Does It Mean to be an INTJ Female? 5
  Profile of an INTJ Female 5
  How Is Being an INTJ Female Different from an INTJ Male? 9
Chapter 2: Female INTJ Development 13
  Understanding Your Childhood 13
  Outward Attitude and Appearance 17
Chapter 3: Education and the INTJ Female 21
  Classroom Behavior 21
  Learning Outside the Classroom 26
Chapter 4: Female INTJ Friendships and Interests .. 28
  Making Friends 28
  Hobbies and Interests 32
Chapter 5: Female INTJ on the Job 35
  Career Paths and Preferences 35
  Jack of All Trades 39
Chapter 6: Relationships and Parenting for the INTJ Woman 42
  What Do We Need in a Partner? 42
  Parenting Style as an INTJ Mother 47
Chapter 7: Strengths and Weaknesses of the INTJ Woman 50
  Strengths 50
  Wrapping Things Up 51
About the Expert 53
Recommended Resources 53

Chapter 1: What Does It Mean to be an INTJ Female?

Profile of an INTJ Female

So you're an INTJ female? Congratulations, you're part of the less than 1% of the population with that title. You've likely been misunderstood your whole life and probably haven't met another woman like yourself. From the outside looking in we are the solo woman in the corner of the coffee shop reading a book. We are the employee eating lunch at our desk or in our car rather than in the break room. You're the one with a to-do list for each day and your grocery list is organized by department. We wear our minimalistic black/white/grey wardrobe proudly and don't spend time on stereotypical female activities like shopping and gossiping, and we have very few friends. To the outsider we're the woman that has a death stare and our gaze can be both piercing and look right through a person. As an INTJ woman you slightly scare and intimidate people. Others think we are void of emotion: they will never know otherwise unless we choose to share this with them. When we INTJ women speak we have carefully analyzed all the facts and precede to list, in detail, all the reasons someone is wrong (the list is long).

On the inside we have much more going on than just being an anti-social book worm. As an INTJ woman we are highly intelligent and love learning about anything that sparks interest. We are highly strategic and always have a contingency plan and think at least 10 steps ahead. We can quickly put together pieces of information from the past along with new information to form a conclusion. This means we can often predict the outcome of events and often mutter, "I told you so". We are very analytical and enjoy finding out the why and how behind everything. The INTJ woman thrives on organization and planning; we don't enjoy spur of the moment changes which can lead to us turning down last minute invitations. You strive for efficiency in all areas of life and believe only you can do the best job, taking control of situations. While we appear quiet we have dozens of conversations in our head each day; we're also not shy, we just need alone time to recharge because socializing is draining. There is no grey area for the INTJ female and we base decisions off of facts rather than feelings.

The elusive INTJ female: we are few and far from the stereotypical female. We are difficult for others to understand since we break traditional female ideals. But by learning more about yourself you'll realize your personality type is unique but perfectly acceptable.

What Does INTJ Stand For?

All these letters and no idea what they mean? So quick run-down of what INTJ actually stands for and means. The "I" is for introverted. This is how we gain our energy. We INTJ ladies thrive on alone time and can feel drained after too much human contact. We need time to be alone, recharge, and process emotions without others present. When an INTJ woman says her plans for the day are nothing...it means we actually plan on doing nothing, not that our schedules are open. We need that alone time.

The "N" actually stands for intuition (weird, but there couldn't be two I's I suppose). This refers to the way the INTJ woman takes in information. We take in information and process it internally. We're not the type that needs to talk things out. We makes decisions based off gut feelings and quickly align new information with old information. We also tend to make decisions based off of previous experiences. Example: screw us once and we'll likely always assume you'll do it again. None of that mushy second chance stuff. Intuition is how an INTJ woman can tell what's going to happen next and usually mutters, "told you so".

The "T" is for thinking. We make decisions based off of facts and logic rather than fuzzy feelings and consideration for others. It's not that we're cold hearted, we really do have feelings. But when it comes to making important decisions we like to look at the facts: the things that are tried and true. Making decisions based on feelings (insert cringe) leads to choices based on comfort, not on practicality. And we need practicality.

Finally, the "J" is for judging. This is related to what we do with the information we've obtained. Our brains are hardwired to categorize, sort, and file away information neatly and this is exactly what we do with each new fact. The INTJ woman is constantly comparing new information to old information, making connections at amazing speed. Although we are quick to piece information together, our judging side means we enjoy sticking to a plan and aren't one to improvise at the last minute.

In case you're curious (and since you're an INTJ woman I know you are) here's what the other letters stand for: extraversion, sensing, feeling, and perceiving. Obviously the opposites of us INTJ ladies.

How Is Being an INTJ Female Different from an INTJ Male?

It might not seem immediately obvious that there are key differences between male INTJs and female INTJs. We're both part of the same personality category, right? True. Both male and female INTJs exhibit the same personality traits, but the key difference between the two is how the world perceives and judges these traits. We're all familiar with stereotypes: simply put, stereotypes are general ideas that apply to some but not all members of a group, but are generalized as common traits held by all members of that group. We female INTJs tend to break all the stereotypes for women, and we're proud of it. What is "ok" for males to do is not always socially normal for females to do: and honestly people just don't know what to do when we don't fit into their idea of "normal".

Most girls indulge in at least a little gossip, even stereotyped as playing hard to get, dramatic, or coy. The female INTJ is not any of these things. We can't stand when people play games or make things more difficult than need be. Acting difficult for attention annoys us to no end and we have zero tolerance for that. The INTJ woman is blunt and straight to the point, and we don't care to be around people that are anything but that. If we were to explain to someone that we don't like vagueness or games, they would likely not believe us since "all women" are like that. It can be a struggle to get others to understand that we mean what we say, there's no reading between the lines necessary.

We're also not as outwardly emotional as most women (or even some men for that matter). We have plenty of emotions but we keep them to ourselves. It could literally take days for us to process an emotion and slap a label on it, so we definitely don't wear our emotions on our sleeves. Even after we get a grasp on our emotions we likely won't share them with anyone unless necessary. The INTJ woman loves facts and patterns: strong emotions can be disarming since we don't make decisions based on feelings. We're labeled as cold-hearted because we just don't like dealing with emotions: many men don't know what to do with us and many women feel shut down by us.

Women are also stereotyped as compliant and go with the flow. Not us. We INTJ women challenge everything we view as incorrect or unjust. If we think a process could be improved upon, we won't just go along with it because a superior told us to. We will always voice our opinions (if that person is lucky, we may even phrase it in the form of a question instead of flat out telling them their way is inefficient). The INTJ woman doesn't just accept something: we constantly challenge the status quo, look for ways to improve workflow, and demand a logical explanation for everything. One of our favorite things to do is to keep asking someone "why" and make them state in their own words that their logic is wrong; make someone dig their own grave so to speak. We're constantly saying, "I told you so". This leads to people viewing us as arrogant or hard-headed.

The INTJ woman is also very independent. This is due in large part to our introvert tendencies. We don't need (or even want) another person around in order to do things. If we want to go to our favorite restaurant or see the newest movie, we won't think twice about grabbing our purse and heading there solo. It's hard for us to accept help because we see it as a handout that makes us feel dependent (and also makes us feel stupid, nor do we want to owe anyone a favor). We are assertive and will not back down from our beliefs or challenges we encounter: but in a woman assertiveness is often labeled hormonal or dramatic. Partners often don't know what to do with a woman who doesn't really need (or even want) help and our independence is often viewed as being cold and distant. Sometimes our relationships are viewed as backwards: the INTJ woman is the one typically not meeting her partner's emotional needs.

Our interests and knowledge is also similar to typical male interests: we enjoy STEM subjects, independence, logic, we can likely fix a clogged pipe, or can probably figure out how to maintain our own vehicle. We have the confidence to research and tackle almost any project head-on and it takes a lot for us to ask for help. If we do break down and ask for help, we're the women that hover and offer to hand you tools or ask if we can do it while you walk us through it. It takes a special guy to be ok with a woman who doesn't need help (although most friends will think it's so cool how we can tackle anything).

One major difference between we INTJ females and other females is that we are not here to please others. We don't care if other people like us, if we have friends, or if we have plans on Friday night. The opinions of most people do not matter to us. We're not here to be the prettiest, most popular, or social. We're here to learn, take charge, and tackle every obstacle we come across. We are seen as outcasts and loners, although neither label offends us. Other women often don't know what to do with us because our priorities often don't align with theirs. Even if we do find other goal-oriented peers they often don't make decisions based on the same reasons as us or live to the same standards as us.

Many people are intimidated by us INTJ females because we are unpredictable by typical female standards. We don't fit into the idea of a stereotypical female and I've even been called a woman with a male's personality. The characteristics we display aren't uncalled for: but they are more often displayed by men instead of women. One of the biggest obstacles in life for us is that we break the female mold. Men are often intimidated and turned off because they feel emasculated; women are often also intimidated and turned off because they can't relate to us or view us as competition. This often leaves us INTJ women alone until we can find partners and friends who can tolerate our independence, intelligence, and assertiveness.

Chapter 2: Female INTJ Development

Understanding Your Childhood

Childhood is a difficult time for us INTJ females. Making friends, relating to family, and finding our place in the world is a struggle for the young INTJ girl. The whole, "sugar, spice and everything nice" phrase didn't really apply to us as we were inquisitive, literal, and serious. The INTJ girl is often described as an old soul or wise beyond her years.

As a child we often had questions about issues our peers didn't even know existed and challenged the status quo. The INTJ girl is inquisitive and examines the how and why of everything. If we asked our parents a question often times the answer wasn't good enough: we wanted to know the reasoning behind the answer. If my mom told me not to feed the dog grapes, I didn't just accept it and not feed the dog grapes. I wanted to know why they couldn't have grapes. My mom had to call the vet for the answer: there's something in grapes that is toxic to dogs even though it's not toxic to humans (que further questioning about why some things are ok for people to eat but not animals and vice versa). Let's just say my mom spent a lot of time with me at the library.

We did not accept something just because an adult told us. The phrase, "because I said so" was not a sufficient answer for us nor did we respect and obey an adult just because they were older than us. The young INTJ is highly perceptive and can quickly pick up on character and trustworthiness of others. We easily picked up on the vibe we felt from others. Our minds did, and still do, process and link pieces of information together very quickly: if something you said last year doesn't align with your actions or something you just said, we will immediately have doubts and lose trust (and probably call you out on it). We didn't care what an adult told us to do, if we felt it was wrong we couldn't do it. The INTJ girl is very literal and doesn't appreciate or participate in vagueness or ambiguity. The INTJ girl is often called argumentative but really we are just analytical and inquisitive. The INTJ girl has a very high IQ and is a perfectionist. Our analytical nature leads us to research, read books, and seek information wherever possible.

The young INTJ female is very independent and needs a great deal of alone time. Our independence is rooted in the knowledge that we are intelligent and capable of making decisions on our own. This is good because as a young INTJ making friends could be incredibly difficult. As a child we had zero tolerance for immaturity or stupidity in peers and found it easy to end friendships. Part of the reason we value alone time is that being an introvert means socializing drains us. As a young INTJ, this means we were more likely to be reading or drawing instead of playing with other kids. We were mature for our age and didn't have the patience for loud, obnoxious kids: we thrived on a quiet place to retreat by ourselves. Being different from our peers often lead to being bullied. Other children simply didn't understand us and that likely lead to being picked on or left out. While it sounds like a rough childhood, this was the foundation for our adult lives as intelligent, independent, and introverted INTJ women.

Internal Struggles

Let's face it: we INTJ women have a lot going on in our minds because we're constantly taking in and processing information. Most struggles the INTJ woman will face will be dealt with internally; sharing personal issues and talking things out are not our style. Once we are hit with a certain emotion, we could retreat away for hours or even days to decode what the exact feeling is we are experiencing (we don't act quickly just because of an emotion we experience). Most people would say they are mad; the INTJ woman says to herself, "I need to go be alone, process, and label this negative emotion I am feeling". Eight hours later it will suddenly dawn on us, "oh! I'm not mad, I'm jealous!". The rational aspect of our personality allows us to realize there is more than simply being mad, but rather there is an underlying, very specific name for what we are feeling. We just need an hour or 12 to put a name to that emotion.

Many of our internal struggles are due to the fact that we have the rarest personality combination: a woman with an INTJ personality. I've heard finding an INTJ woman is like finding a unicorn (I'm inclined to believe this is true since I've never encountered another INTJ female). The INTJ personality is made up of characteristics that are generally stereotyped as male: independent, logical, rational, a leader, intelligent, methodical, and even standoffish. With a male these characteristics are usually viewed as masculine or assertive. For an INTJ female, this can lead to less pleasant labels such as cold, arrogant, or rude. We're not emotionless; rather we listen to our rational and judging side in addition to our feelings.

We're not cold; we just prefer listening and processing things internally rather than externally.

Part of being an INTJ female is having a thick skin and not letting other people's misperceptions offend us. Most people will not understand our personality and some might even be repelled. But that's ok because we can shrug it off and function just fine on our own, as usual.

Outward Attitude and Appearance

There's so much going on in our heads that it's easy to forget about the impression we make upon others. Let's be honest, you probably don't care what anyone thinks of you and you never will. We are not people-pleasers. To others, this can come across as cold or rude. The INTJ woman doesn't see the point of gossip or talking for the sake of making noise. Small talk is unbearable: we view it as a strange and unnecessary social norm. INTJ women have perfected the poker face and it's almost impossible for others to perceive what we are thinking or feeling. While it appears that we are zoned out and disinterested, we're really analyzing every aspect of what's being said for information and accuracy. If something entirely incorrect is said, the INTJ woman will likely speak up with the correct answer and shock everyone that she was even listening.

The problem arises when we're in a social situation and don't respond in the same way as other women. When the rest of the group is laughing and sharing stories, you're sitting there with a straight face and analyzing everything that's being said, but you're not saying much. By not participating in the situation in a way that is socially normal, people conclude that we don't care about what's being said or don't care about the people present. What's hard to understand is that we won't interject unless what we have to say will add substance to the conversation: but the lack of engagement can appear cold.

I've found that this isn't a huge problem with my immediate family and friends, but rather an issue I have with acquaintances and colleagues. When people know you well, they come to anticipate the above behavior from you, although they may not fully understand your reasoning. If someone calls me out on my lack of participation, I simply tell them I am more of a listener and throw in a little head nod here and there during conversation to show I'm actively paying attention.

A young INTJ girl will encounter the same issues but with a different twist. As a child, the INTJ girl is likely to struggle making friends their own age simply because children don't understand how to react when others don't behave in the way society tells us they should. While other kids like to play by creating unrealistic pretend scenarios and giving toys fake voices and personalities, the INTJ girl loves books, learning, and asking questions. The young INTJ isn't loud, doesn't interrupt, and is very mature for her age. This leads the young INTJ girl to feel more comfortable talking to adults rather than kids her own age: adults are a source of knowledge, more understanding, and seem to appreciate the level of maturity displayed by the young INTJ.

INTJ girls are often labeled book worms, know-it-alls, old souls, mature for their age, and highly intelligent. As a young child these labels can be hurtful for the INTJ girl: but as we age we learn to embrace our strengths and differences. We turn to books or solo activities rather than peers for entertainment and become more secure in our individuality.

As an adult, I'm guilty of sitting in a group of people who are chatting away but I myself am silent. The questions never end: are you ok, do you feel ill, what's wrong? Nothing is wrong; I just enjoy observing and analyzing the exchange rather than participating (what I'd actually prefer is to be sitting at home reading a book or organizing my house…). I've been called a buzzkill, know-it-all, arrogant, uptight, and boring among other things. I don't find these labels hurtful; rather I see these words as a reflection of the person that said them and their ignorance.

Part of the way we communicate with the world is through our appearance. As an INTJ woman you likely have a functional, minimalistic, and small wardrobe. A capsule wardrobe is the INTJ woman's best friend: the no-fuss simplicity is right up our alley. A few staple pieces that transcend seasons are the foundation of your flexible, classic wardrobe. We tend to favor black, white, and grey pieces as they are easily mixed and provide many combinations. A pop of color or hue of the season is not something we care about and we won't be found browsing fashion magazines or shopping for fun.

A Little Black Dress is a staple in my closet: I have three of them and all three can be dressed up or down depending on the day. Clothes that are multipurpose like this make up the majority of the INTJ woman's wardrobe. The clothes we wear don't call attention to ourselves and fits with the reality that an INTJ woman does an excellent job of observing but not being seen. It's been said that your clothes say a lot about you: the INTJ woman's clothes reflect that she is practical, no-fuss, and un-swayed by outside influence.

A couple of years ago I decided to streamline my closet and create a minimalistic capsule wardrobe. It felt nice getting rid of all the clothes I had acquired that I didn't love nor wear. I kept all my favorite pieces and over time bought a handful of new items that allowed me to mix up the clothes I had to create new outfits. Pretty much everything in my closet is either black, white, or grey. I have a couple of blue and denim pieces and shoes that go with almost any outfit. Picking an outfit out is effortless (which I love) because all my pieces are interchangeable and I don't have to spend an hour putting an outfit together. Fashion doesn't mean much to me so I love my no-fuss closet and my black and white "uniform".

Chapter 3: Education and the INTJ Female

Classroom Behavior

The INTJ girl has one of the highest IQs (INTJs in general are thought to have the highest IQs) and are at the top of their class. We can be seen as know-it-alls, which can drive our peers insane and make us very unpopular. Learning is an actual hobby and passion for us: it's not that it comes easy to us but rather we devote ourselves to it. The INTJ female might not be valedictorian (because she loses interest if not challenged or doesn't care about a particular class), but are among the most intelligent of their class. It is possible that the INTJ girl skips a grade or two ahead of her peers due to her intelligence and maturity.

The INTJ girl is the quiet student in the classroom, preferring to listen first and ask questions as they arise rather than speaking out of turn. Teachers may assume that the quiet INTJ girl is day dreaming or not paying attention when in reality they are just observing and intently listening. I've had teachers accuse me of being lazy when in reality INTJ girls just can't be bothered to focus on anything they don't find interesting. It's hard to ask us to spend energy learning about something we find uninteresting, or more commonly, something we find redundant (example: why do we have gym class? Who doesn't know that we need exercise? If I was interested in a particular sport I'd play it on my own, thanks). If we are not passionate about the topic then teachers will have a very hard time getting us to focus and learn about a particular topic.

We INTJ females absolutely despise group projects. No one can live up to our standards of quality and to be blunt, we don't want to waste time collaborating with other people when we could just do it right by ourselves the first time. Group projects force us to socialize and pretend that others' work is as descent as ours. I'd be lying if I said I never told a group to give me their pieces and I'll assemble the project...just because I wanted to screen the information and make it as best as possible. The INTJ female is a perfectionist at heart and can't stand half-hearted attempts. Often times the INTJ girl is bullied because she is different from everyone else. In the beginning this is difficult, but eventually normal and embraced.

The INTJ female sees school as a means to an end: meaning we know that school is necessary in order to progress in the world but we don't necessarily enjoy suffering through it. Most people would assume that school is a paradise for the intellectual INTJ girl. However, the way school is structured overwhelms and annoys us. The young INTJ girl is smart enough to realize that traditional schooling tests your memory, not your knowledge. But we realize we have to endure this if we intend on going to college, obtaining a career, and making a difference in the world. Traditional schooling is annoying to us for many reasons. We don't fit in with our female peer which is incredibly frustrating for a young INTJ girl that hasn't embraced her differences. We also don't learn at the same pace or in the same way as our peers. The INTJ girl learns many subjects at a mind-blowing pace; other subjects she muddles through due to lack of interest or because teachers are unable to answer the fundamental "but why" question. We need sources, facts and data. It's very difficult for us to just accept something because it is taught to us. The INTJ girl can't stand when a teacher is unable to explain the fundamentals of a subject: telling isn't an option, the logic needs to be explained. If a teacher can't do this, the INTJ girl will become frustrated and distant.

Regardless of grade level the INTJ female finds school to be draining. As an introvert, it's taxing to have to be around people all day, to be called on to speak, and to be forced to be someplace you don't want to be. School leads us into a state of anxiety, depression and can even make us physically sick. Online school is a blessing to us INTJ women: we're able to learn at our own pace without the burden of peers, incompetent teachers, and anxiety. Between the negative social interaction and bullying, school was my worst nightmare. I enjoyed learning: I researched on my own and did plenty of learning at home. But I hated dragging myself to school every day just to be misunderstood, slow my pace for others, or spend time on things I didn't view as necessary. Online school was a new option at the time and I begged my parents to let me quit my uptight Catholic school for this choice but I was unsuccessful. At first I was little and would go to the nurse and say I was sick. This wasn't a lie: I was truly ill but I didn't understand was anxiety was, I just thought I was sick to my stomach or had a fever. In high school I understood what was happening and I rebelled: I began spending one period each day as an assistant for the school office. This meant I got my own desk and besides running a few errands I was left alone. This also meant I was privy to the truancy rules. I knew exactly how many days I could miss each quarter without facing disciplinary action from the school and state. At this point I suffered from anxiety and depression and my parents were aware of this: if I told them I needed a mental health day they were ok with it as long as I wasn't missing something vital or close to being truant. The reality was that after so many days of being around classmates that drained me and teachers/courses that bored me I needed a day to myself. I needed to wake up on my own, drink a cup of coffee, and do something that calmed my spirit. I always felt surrounded by idiots and sometimes I just needed a break from it all.

Subjects That We Enjoy...and Ones We Don't

As an INTJ girl we were often labeled nerds, which actually didn't bother us. We have a deep love for learning and there are only few topics we will turn away from. While there is always an exception to the rule, generally speaking INTJ females prefer STEM subjects and other logical topics over most others. Grade school and even high school can be difficult because we are forced to study certain subjects that we may not be passionate about. This is draining and can lead the INTJ girl to dislike going to school. But the ability to choose classes that interest us will fuel our passion for learning and make school a favorite place.

We love all science topics: physics, astronomy, geology, and biology to name a few. Science appeals to us because while there are infinite questions there are also answers if we dig deep enough. Science and research provides answers for all of the universe's questions and this deeply appeals to our logical side. For the same reasons technology/engineering appeals to us, in addition to allowing us to create solutions and efficiency.

The INTJ female also enjoys history: we believe that it's important to know where we came from and what happened so we can learn from the past and improve the future. History is facts and facts make us comfortable. We also enjoy debating the "why" surrounding history: why people made the choices they did. That's also the reason why psychology appeals to us. We love learning what makes people tick and feel that it gives us an advantage to know what others are thinking (we've also been called psychic a time or two, but really we just pay close attention and are excellent at reading others).

As an INTJ woman we have the ability to apply ourselves to any subject and be successful. However, we have a difficult time applying ourselves to anything that we aren't passionate about. Vague subjects like music or creative writing can be difficult for us to enjoy (although technical or persuasive writing can be enjoyable). Math can be a struggle for the INTJ girl because there's nothing left to be done so to speak. Math is just spinning your wheels: it's already been figured out, there's not much new ground to break and we don't enjoy pointless activities.

While none of this may seem problematic for a female INTJ, the topics we enjoy are predominately male-preferred subjects. As we get a little older it can be difficult to find female friends at school who enjoy the same things we do. This also steers us towards more male-dominated career paths, such as STEM careers. Since our interests don't align with many females, school can be a lonely time for us: we just want to go to school, learn, and leave any drama at the door.

Learning Outside the Classroom

The INTJ woman is in constant pursuit of knowledge and learning doesn't end after college. The desire to learn is hardwired into our brains and we will never feel we are finished with education. We often choose career paths that require continued education courses, such as veterinarians, doctors, or other professions where professional credits are necessary (these careers align with our interests and just happen to require constant additional learning).

We INTJ women love to dive into research projects. Whenever we come across an interesting topic we could spend anywhere from hours to weeks researching the ins and outs of it. There's no such thing as just casually looking into a topic. At first we just do some online searching and then before you know it we're curled up on the couch with a stack of books and taking notes. If it involves researching a skill, you better believe we've already made a trip to the hardware or craft store

As an INTJ woman we also indulge in some short courses or side classes for fun: online courses where you can get a certificate are one of our favorite things ever. It's highly likely that you have a random certification in something like creative writing, glass blowing, or photography. You're proud of your random skills and are always looking for new opportunities to add to your list.

We can often be found in bookstores or libraries and we see browsing them as legitimate hobbies. We could curl up in the corner chair with a book and get lost in the information. It's similar with museums and exhibits: we're the people that have to stop and read every placard and spend the entire day there. Thankfully, these are activities we can do alone because not many friends/partners want to spend an entire day at the library or museum (and we're perfectly ok with this). INTJ women also hate to ask for help but when we do, we prefer that you show us rather than do it for us. If we need help repairing a hole in the drywall and you offer to do it for us, we'll counteroffer by asking you to supervise and walk us through how to do it ourselves. We struggle with having things done for us.

By spending all this time researching, we INTJ females end up knowing a little bit about (almost) everything. The downside of this is that we can come across as know-it-alls to people that don't understand us. We don't speak often but will chime in if something incorrect is said in conversation. This can be annoying: people think we're only interested in correcting them (...sort of true). We just have a serious problem with overhearing incorrect statements without setting the record straight.

Chapter 4: Female INTJ Friendships and Interests

Making Friends

The bottom line for INTJ females when it comes to friends is quality over quantity. We would prefer to have one or two deep, meaningful friendships than 10 trivial ones. As with all other aspects of our lives, we have high standards when it comes to what we look for and tolerate in a friend. As an INTJ female I'm not looking for someone only interested in gossip and surface level interests: I'm looking for a friend who is loyal and intellectual. We tend to look for friendships that challenge us to think, discuss different viewpoints, and are intellectually stimulating.

As a female this can raise several challenges. The most obvious challenge being we will likely never find another INTJ female to befriend, the odds are just not in our favor. Second best would be befriending an INTJ male (or really any intellectually stimulating type) but this can create new issues. Partners of both the INTJ female and male could become jealous, other women are caught off guard when an INTJ female is able to maintain a platonic relationship with males, and sometimes males just don't know how to react when challenged by the INTJ woman. By challenging a male's logic or ideals there are really only two options: he will be fascinated and enjoy carrying on an interesting conversation with you or he will be completely caught off guard by a female with such a strong personality and not enjoy being challenged. In my experience the former has been the most common occurrence. Males have seemed to enjoy a non-stereotypical female who is interested in deep conversation and moral debates.

It's incredibly difficult to befriend an INTJ female, but once you do we will be a fiercely loyal friend to the end. We are the friend you call when you need help with a tricky situation and we're always there (and on time, shocker). We struggle to listen without giving advice, because who would want to just vent? Surely this friend is looking for a solution? This is one area where the INTJ woman could focus on improving. It's difficult for us to understand, but some people want to just vent without being told how to fix a problem. Weird, right? But having an INTJ girl friend can be highly valuable, as we are often 10 steps ahead and can see all aspects of a situation, offering solutions for every possible scenario so you can make the best decision. As a loner and introvert, we value friendships that are not clingy. We still enjoy our independence and can actually go long periods of time without communicating with our friends and then pick back up like no time had passed. Our friends have to be ok with dry, dark humor and sarcasm: sometimes a sarcastic comment falls out of our mouths before we even realize it. If others find this off-putting, oh well. Bottom line: if we INTJ females allow someone into our lives it's because we want them there, not because we need them. We will also disengage from a friendship when we feel it has run its course.

So how have we managed to find any friends? Usually we get adopted by a persistent extrovert that we can't seem to shake, but they're a descent mix of independent and intelligent so we allow them to balance our social lives a little. I can honestly say that all my friendships have started because 1. I admired someone's intelligence or wit and paid them a sincere compliment or 2. I was adopted by a tolerable and understanding extrovert. Almost all my friendships throughout school were with males and I still struggle to find common ground with the majority of females. Some of the best friendships I've had throughout the years were with people who had totally different beliefs than me and we debated just for the sake of it. I've had amazing friendships where we're both content to sit in the same room reading two different books. I've also had friendships where we go years without seeing one another but are able to start a conversation like no time has passed. Do I have any friends right now? Yup, my dog and cat of course.

Introvert of All Introverts

As an INTJ woman one of our most basic needs is the need to be alone. Extroverts get their energy from being around people while introverts obtain their energy from alone time. Do you find yourself in need of a nap or a day to yourself after attending a social gathering? Does it take you 8 hours of talking to yourself before you can feel psychologically able to attend a party? Does your enthusiasm and patience wear thin the longer you're at the gathering? Does just being in the presence of other people, like at the grocery store, make you feel exhausted? This is the introvert aspect of our personalities.

As an INTJ woman you've probably been called "too quiet" before or constantly asked if something is wrong. Unless it's a fellow "I – introvert" type, most people don't understand that we're fine: we're just processing things internally while extroverts process things externally. As a woman, our "thinking face" is constantly mistaken for a bad attitude and we're accused of being unhappy. People generally anticipate women will be outgoing and engage happily in conversation, but that's just not us. The INTJ woman is usually happiest and most comfortable alone, away from obligatory small talk and social interactions.

Finding a long term partner and friends who accept and embrace this aspect of our personality type can be difficult. I've told my husband to go to gatherings without me and I've even asked for him to please go find something to do so I can recharge and be alone. The conversation usually goes, "I need you to take me home so I can make food and then go to sleep: I've had too much people-time today". Thankfully he understands. No matter how much you love the people in your life, you need personal time and space. An INTJ woman who is worn out from socializing can be snappy and bitter until able to decompress.

What are some ways to take care of your introverted self? Don't schedule more than you can handle. If you have two meetings, lunch with your mother, and a presentation to give it is completely acceptable (and probably in your best interest) to pass up happy hour with coworkers. Realizing your maximum socializing abilities will keep you from overcommitting and winding up stressed and cranky. Realize that it's ok to say no. As women we're often taught that we must be polite in every situation and saying anything other than yes to an invitation is rude. If the thought of going to a karaoke bar makes you sweat, say "no thank you" and hopefully they won't ask you to go ever again. If you're invited to dinner and a movie but are overbooked this week, feel free to suggest an alternate day. No matter what you have going on each day, make sure to do something that recharges you so you don't wear yourself out.

Hobbies and Interests

A large part of caring of yourself as an introvert is taking time to recharge. Although we female INTJs don't enjoy many of the social interactions of a stereotypical female, we still need a way to pass the time doing something enjoyable. When I realized I needed a hobby I started looking at the definition of what a hobby is: basically it's an activity that you regularly do in your spare time for your pleasure. We tend to enjoy hobbies that we can do by ourselves: photography, working out, gardening, reading, and even learning (yup as long as it's your free time and you enjoy it, it's considered a hobby).

I realized every hobby I do speaks to my INTJ personality: they are solo (or minimal interaction), educational, and make me feel refreshed and recharged. I have a few activities that I would consider hobbies but I absolutely love hiking: I live for the adventure of new places, pushing myself physically, seeing beautiful views, and learning new skills. I spend more time planning and researching a hike than I actually spend on the trail itself. I love researching new places and coming up with itineraries (basically I love organization). I could spend weeks researching new gear and practicing with it, coming up with packing lists, and booking accommodations. I find the research and planning part to be entirely relaxing and enjoyable. Full disclosure: I've planned out trips that we haven't even taken yet.

I also enjoy photography. My hiking adventures allow me the opportunity to take beautiful photographs. I took a film photography class in high school and have been hooked ever since. My husband was kind enough to convert an unused bathroom into a darkroom so I could process film. At home I enjoy gardening although my flower bed definitely does not look like it's straight out of a magazine. It might not be perfectly manicured, but I love researching what each plant needs to thrive and watching my efforts pay off.

Every hobby I enjoy is based on solitude and research. To me, digging into a subject and learning as much as possible is entertaining and speaks to my female INTJ traits. We seek knowledge and mastery of everything we try. We don't half-commit to anything: we give every project our all even if it means late nights online just for the sake of learning a trivial skill. Our love of knowledge means we often look into random topics and this leads us to being relatively educated in many topics.

Since hobbies like these are considered antisocial, others might not know how to process this information. I often explain my interests only to be asked if I get bored or what I do for fun. Actually everything I listed is what I do for fun and no I do not miss people, thanks for asking. People related to one another based on common interests and it can be difficult to find others who enjoy or appreciate solo hobbies. Regardless of what other people think, continue to pursue hobbies and interests that you enjoy and bring you a sense of relief from everyday life.

Chapter 5: Female INTJ on the Job

Career Paths and Preferences

INTJ females can excel at any job we set our minds too. However we obviously have our preferences. While STEM careers (science, technology, engineering, math) tend to be heavily male populated, INTJ women often excel in these areas as well. Even if we do not enter into a STEM profession, we INTJ women prefer a workplace that allowed for creativity and responsibility. Doing the same repetitive task over and over will drive us insane. We also can't stand jobs where we're required to perform trivial tasks below our means, as that is almost humiliating.

The INTJ woman will thrive in a work environment where allowed to be creative, design and implement new system, and make improvements to existing organizational structures. We would prefer to work independently or with minimal supervision. If necessary, we'll work in small teams. In an effort to recruit and retain more millennials some employers have adopted a close knit, friendly workplace (think: beer cart on Fridays, karaoke Wednesdays and work retreats). This is not something the INTJ woman seeks: in fact we find it rather bizarre and unnecessary.

The INTJ woman has the mindset that work and social life are two different things and should not intersect. If we have a friend, it is most likely not a colleague of ours. We also have an issue with colleagues who do not do their fair share of work but receive equal recognition, or worse, a promotion.

As innovative as we are, we prefer to have a structured work environment with set responsibilities. We do not like vague positions like, "assistant with possible admin and accounting responsibilities". No. We like clearly defined job descriptions and duties and then we can spend our time practicing and improving our position. Yes we are constantly looking to gain new skills and advance in our careers. But a whisy-washy list of responsibilities sends up red flags for the INTJ female and gives us a negative impression of that employer. If the employer can't clearly articulate the position then how can I effectively do my job? The INTJ woman has no patience for scattered business practices and incompetency.

The INTJ woman has the potential to thrive in positions that are often male dominated such as IT, researcher, engineer, entrepreneur, or lawyer are excellent options. While there are many fields that the INTJ can thrive in, most tend to be male-dominated. Ant INTJ woman in the right field could find that, although females in these positions are rarer, they are surrounded by like-minded individuals. Finding coworkers who are just as driven, responsible, and independent as the female INTJ provides reassurance that they are not alone in the world. While coworkers might not also have the INTJ type, being surrounded by fellow intellectuals can be a relief.

I'll be the first to admit I have worked in dissatisfying jobs that didn't mesh well with my personality type. During my sophomore year of undergrad, my boyfriend (now husband) and I decided to start a tree service. He had been working his whole life for other businesses and he knew how to run a tree service. What he didn't know was how to start a business. I switched up my class schedule, took as many online classes as possible, worked part time in the evenings, and spend my days researching how to legally start a company. My passion ended up being business and I loved growing our business more than I liked my college major. Sure, there have been times we meet new people and explain what we do and they automatically assume my husband is solely responsible for this company. Sometimes that aggravates me, but it's immediately followed with pride as I explain that we created this fantastic business out of thin air. Being an entrepreneur allowed me to push myself and it's amazing to know that we alone are responsible for our success.

Dissatisfaction in the Workplace

Given that the INTJ female is a strong employee who can tackle almost any assignment; it can be difficult to imagine that we can be dissatisfied in the workplace. Dissatisfaction can come from various sources of friction. We often feel that the job we have is beneath us and we're capable of more. As an INTJ female it's easy to feel that our above-and-beyond efforts go unrecognized, which can be discouraging. We work very hard and if someone in the office who lacks gets praised but we don't, this can leave us feeling frustrated and angry since we don't respect those who don't work hard. An INTJ woman is always looking for ways to solve problems and streamline processes. Unfortunately if we are not in a position of authority, many of these ideas are ignored. As an INTJ woman, speaking our opinion regarding inefficiencies or efficiencies can lead to conflict. Generally women are not viewed in a positive manner for sticking to their opinions and not backing down: this can lead to some serious name calling. While a persistent man might be viewed as passionate, a woman could be viewed as stubborn or arrogant.

Dissatisfaction at work can come in many forms. Having to collaborate in teams but do all the work can lead an INTJ woman resentful. Working according to someone else's hours and schedule is annoying. Creating a wonderful way to streamline a process at work but being told no because "don't fix what isn't broken" can leave us bitter. Just having to attend pointless meetings every day instead of sending out a streamlined email will leave us frustrated and annoyed. We don't want to be friends with coworkers and no thanks when it comes to happy hour and karaoke.

The INTJ woman is an incredibly hard worker and can accomplish pretty much any task assigned to her. As I mentioned before, INTJ women make excellent entrepreneurs and often have the thought, "I could do this better and I could do it myself". This leads many female INTJs to quit the 8-6 grind and start their own businesses. By being an entrepreneur we eliminate the frustration associated with incapable coworkers and are able to do things our way/the right way without being told no. Eventually we get tired of working towards someone else's dream and decide to start living our own dream.

I have a laundry list of things that bugged me about my 8-5 job. My boss had no idea what our team actually did, but yet she made decisions on our behalf. Upper management didn't address employee concerns about her incompetence. As the main employee doing a specific function, I would voice my concern over a new procedure and why that new procedure would negatively impact me and in turn the team, only to be told my opinion did not matter. I was drug into management's office numerous times for not being as friendly or social as they would have liked, as our office pushed coworkers to have friendships. Basically that job was one giant example of what leads the INTJ to being dissatisfied at work: suggestions being ignored, incompetent leaders, and being chastised for having an offbeat personality type.

Needless to say, I am no longer at that job. Unless a very unique opportunity comes my way, I think I'll just sit in my home office and manage my little company as I see fit.

Jack of All Trades

The INTJ female is lucky to be considered a jack of all trades. We absolutely love researching various topics, even if it's something we'll probably never use in real life (how do hospitals move the deceased without us seeing? Yup, we know the answer). We are constantly seeking out answers to random questions or researching various skills, as we have an incurable thirst for knowledge. This leads us to find many topics interesting and many jobs an option for us. It can be hard for an INTJ woman to choose a career path, mainly because everything is so interesting and she is able to pick up any skill quickly.

The downside of knowing a little bit about everything is that we can come across as arrogant. We're the first ones to chime in if someone has their facts wrong or if a question is asked and we know the answer. Unfortunately this wears on most people even though we don't intend to come across as a know-it-all. But we love information and hate incorrect statements, so we can't help but state what we know when the opportunity arises.

This raises a problem for us as women, by again, breaking traditional stereotypes. Most women need to "call a guy": a plumber, handyman, or mechanic. We INTJ women don't need to call a guy, we need a few minutes with a computer or book and we've got this handled ourselves. In a relationship it can be awkward for a man to not be needed for things like this and it may take time for them to adjust to having a highly independent woman. It takes a special type of partner and friends to understand our independence and not mistake our knowledge for arrogance.

This interest in all subjects has lead me to pursue jobs in many different areas. I've worked in multiple veterinary offices, sales, entrepreneurship, writing, big pharma...and even jobs in cosmetics and lingerie (uh, yeah I know). I enjoyed even the weird jobs (the cosmetics and lingerie in case you couldn't guess). Both allowed me make people feel beautiful and learn some artistic and fashion skills along the way. I've also pursued countless hobbies: hiking, photography, writing, four wheeling, camping, and sewing to name a few. Anything to add to my skill set works for me.

I am incredibly fortunate to have a mother and father that not only accepted but nurtured my love of knowledge and curiosity for all skills. I was taught how to cook, balance a check book, change the oil in a truck, and back up a trailer among many other skills. Anything I was curious about, my parents showed me how to do it or gave me the tools to research and teach myself. I'm also fortunate to have a husband that appreciates and even admires what I am capable of doing and what I know. I'm grateful he can see that it's not arrogance on my part, but rather a love for knowledge.

Chapter 6: Relationships and Parenting for the INTJ Woman

What Do We Need in a Partner?

I personally believe (due to experience) that the biggest struggle for an INTJ female is finding a life-long partner. As INTJ females we are the most likely to be single. It's incredibly difficult for us to commit to a relationship because we don't settle for just anyone: but once we find our person we commit fully and our relationships are very intense and loyal. There are a few reasons we're voted "most likely to be single"; we are difficult to impress, hard to match in terms of intelligence, and it takes a very special person to realize that we INTJ women have a lot to offer underneath our exterior attitudes.

We are alpha females: we take control of our lives, are assertive, build ourselves up, take risks in pursuit of benefits, and take ownership of creating the life we want. It's easy to see why many partners are intimidated and even turned off by us. Many people don't know what to do with a woman who doesn't "need" anyone. I don't need saving, I don't need to cry or vent my emotions to you on a daily basis, nor do I need to be touchy-feely (eww). It's very difficult for us to admit that we need or want another person in our lives.

Generally speaking it's a very persistent person that will win our affection. We might be told that we're in a relationship before we even want or realize it. While we might be among the most intelligent types, we can be a bit oblivious. I have had to be told that someone is flirting with me or that I am dating someone...seriously. It's not just being persistent though, it has to be a person that intellectually and emotionally meets our needs. I remember in high school a guy had been...talking to/dating...I'm not sure...told me he called my school and was allowed to go to my homecoming dance and he had rented a suit and needed to know what color tie to get. Ummm no. I shut that down immediately. I ignored him for a week and then sent him a text saying please stop calling, I'm not interested. Cold? Ehh maybe. But there's a difference between being pushy and appreciating the INTJ female. My husband on the other hand pursued my mind: he wanted my opinions, to know what I cared about, and allowed me to challenge his viewpoints while challenging mine...he pursued even when I said, "cool, but that doesn't impress me". I fought back every step of the way, but he loved that I didn't just accept his opinion and roll with it. I let him know I didn't need nor did I seek him out (we stumbled upon each other and he just never gave up). Pushy will get someone an immediate dismissal; intrigued and appreciative will land an INTJ female.

It's likely that we will need an extroverted partner. There's a saying about similarities attracting, but we need a partner that is actually the opposite of us externally. We need someone that believes the same things as us but can compensate in the social areas where we lack. We need a partner that has the same core values as we do but can compensate in social situations and other areas where we lack.

We INTJ women are fiercely loyal in relationships and we need a partner that is too. Once we find our person, we are completely devoted and allow them a sneak peek of our softer side. The first act of betrayal is the last: we have zero tolerance for it and don't give second chances. INTJ women need a partner that is driven and has their own goals. Our partners don't have to have a five year plan like we do: but they need to at least have a general idea what they want and be willing to do whatever it takes.

While we need someone that expresses emotion better than we do, we can't handle an emotionally unstable partner. Our partners need to be emotionally mature and in charge of how they respond to their feelings. We need to be able to name, categorize, and set our emotions aside to be dealt with at the right time. It's a real chore to be with someone whose emotions are not in check. Partners can (and should) be emotional, but need to be level headed as well.

Our partners need to be rather open-minded. We're a bit unconventional in our beliefs and enjoy challenging the beliefs of others. As long as there's a logical reason for someone's choice (even if it's not what we choose to believe ourselves) we can accept just about anything. We need a partner that is strong enough to handle the fact we often have unpopular opinions, appreciate different viewpoints even if we disagree with them, and are ok with us being argumentative. At the same time we need a partner with a good sense of humor since sarcasm is our second language. A partner that is easily offended or can't understand when we are or aren't being sarcastic won't last long. Better yet, we'd love a partner that responds in sarcasm as well.

INTJ women need a partner that is mature enough to admit when they are wrong. We can't stand people who refuse to budge when they've been presented with proof that they are incorrect. We need a partner that is secure enough to admit they are wrong when we present them with facts. This shows they are mature but also that they value us. Ultimately our partner needs to be able to keep up with us mentally and in terms of goals. We admire people who push us to be our best and reach our own goals, but at the same time have their own priorities. We aren't clingy nor do we need a clingy partner. Ideally we are two independent people who do something each day to get close to their goals, and when we come home at the end of the day we have a loving partner waiting to hear all about our day.

Being an INTJ Wife

Being an INTJ wife is a strange adventure. We are the most loyal of partners but also the most challenging to understand. Having an INTJ wife is committing to a lifetime of being challenged, reaching new goals, and being pushed to be the best. If someone is looking for a quiet, go-with-the-flow, people pleaser…they need not apply to marry an INTJ woman. While many of us could be happy being stay at home moms, many/most choose to continue pursuing their careers as well as parenthood. We're definitely not the stereotypical wife (think 1950's style). Sure, we may cook and clean but we also expect our spouses to carry their own weight. Labeling something "woman's work" is a great way to start an argument…and we'll whip out the power point slides and bullet pointed list containing all the reasons our spouses should do their share. We are equals in the marriage and expect to be treated as such.

As an INTJ wife you're deeply devoted to your spouse, so you do look for ways to make them feel special. We enjoy making our spouses feel loved, although we don't center our whole day around that. One of the quickest ways to enrage an INTJ wife is to tell her to do something. Ask politely, but don't tell us what to do. Telling us to do something is the fastest way to get us to never do it. Essentially, "I would have done that but then you told me to". On the flip side, INTJ wives have a hard time asking for anything: we're used to doing everything ourselves so asking for anything isn't normal. Well, we also don't ask because we feel no one can do anything as well as we can.

An INTJ wife thrives best when her spouse is the opposite of her in the best possible ways. An extrovert who cares about people and feelings makes a great match. It's been said that the perfect match of MBTI types is an INTJ and ENFP (I agree, but I'm biased since my husband is an ENFP). Essentially these two types project something different to the outside world but recognize that what lies underneath the other's surface is much more complex. The INTJ brings logic and facts to the table while the ENFP brings feelings and people skills among other things. The goals of these two types are incredibly similar, but the strengths they use to get there are quite different. The INTJ wife can balance out her spouse by reminding them to consider the facts and past actions, while their spouse can remind the INTJ wife that our decisions impact the way people feel (and that sometimes we should consider that).

Essentially it's a special type of person that can breach our INTJ walls; let alone enjoy what they find once they're "in". We're difficult, non-stereotypical wives. We stand our own: we don't need a spouse to speak up for or defend us, as we're perfectly capable of handling that on our own. Whoever marries an INTJ woman must realize that independence and space are necessities for us, it's not that we don't enjoy the company of our partner. Marrying an INTJ woman means being challenged every step of the way: if we admit you're right, consider yourself lucky and respected. While it sounds like a chore, having an INTJ wife means lifelong loyalty, humor, and an amazing teammate.

Parenting Style as an INTJ Mother

As I mentioned before, while there are some exceptions to the rule, INTJs are not typically stay at home moms. Trying to balance work, kids, and ourselves can be very straining. We require a lot of alone time to process feelings and to recharge, but having kids alters this. Kids require almost constant attention and undivided attention: while we can do this, we sometimes end up feeling guilty for wanting more alone time or not giving our kids our focused attention. We INTJ women already put our emotional and even physical needs on the back burner and having kids can add to that neglect. We will put our kids first and ourselves further and further down the list of priorities…insert more guilt and frustration.

One of the ways we show love to our kids is by giving and doing the best for them. We're always looking for a way to improve their lives. This doesn't necessarily mean purchasing stuff for our kids: it can mean allowing them to choose what movie we go see, what color they'd like to paint their room, or we'll stay up late getting lunch and backpacks ready so the kids can sleep in a few extra minutes in the morning. We INTJ women are horrible at small talk – we absolutely dread it. This can be weird in situations where kids are together and the parents are expected to interact. We don't want to hear what's going on with other moms; we just want to watch our kid play soccer. On that note, we are incredibly devoted to our kids' events. We're the parents that are at every game, on time, and with all the right gear. We aren't overly concerned with winning or losing: rather we tell our kids to do their best and have fun. If they're no longer enjoying something, then we encourage them to pursue new interests.

Since us INTJ women are pretty unique, we encourage our kids to march to the beat of their own drum. If our toddler insists on dressing herself as a princess when you head to the grocery store, that's fine by us (we likely did the same thing as kids). We're not concerned with fitting into the "normal" standards so we don't mind if our kids are a little offbeat either, we just encourage them to be true to themselves. While most parents forbid talking back and say, "because I told you so", we aren't this way. We encourage our kids that if they disagree with something to ask questions and politely voice their opinions. We try very hard to teach our kids that screaming and crying doesn't work, but using your words to calmly and politely discuss something will get better results. In the long run we are teaching our kids to identify, process, and handle emotions without allowing feelings to become all-consuming.

While we are parents and obviously teach our children, we also acknowledge that they teach us as well. It's likely that our kids won't be INTJs, which means we are teaching and learning from other personality types. Our kids teach us how to relate better to others, exercise patience, and to better roll with whatever comes our way.

Chapter 7: Strengths and Weaknesses of the INTJ Woman

Strengths

Not to brag, but we INTJ women have a lot of strengths on our resume. We are highly organized and constantly seek ways to improve standard processes. We are intelligent and constantly in pursuit of education and learning new skills. We are incredibly responsible and detail-oriented. As an INTJ woman we are open-minded to new concepts and ideas: we enjoy being challenged and (as long as it's logical) accept others' beliefs even if they differ from our own. Our partners will receive unconditional support and loyalty that is incomparable to any other personality type. We take friendships and relationships very seriously and do not play with the emotions of others. We are fantastic listeners since we spend the majority of our time listening, picking up on subtle cues others may not even realize they display. Doing the bare minimum isn't our thing and we almost always go above and beyond what is expected of us. As INTJ women we are always thinking several steps ahead and can often predict an outcome ahead of time, therefore taking steps to achieve the best results. As wives we are intensely loyal and as parents we are very supportive and open-minded.

Weaknesses

Oh man, this one is difficult for us INTJ women to talk about...weaknesses. We don't prefer to show ours to anyone nor do we find it acceptable to have any. While many of the traits associated with us we don't view as weak (rather we see them as entirely normal) society tends to view our non-stereotypical preferences as negatives. It's very rare that someone will witness us INTJ women doing something we don't feel entirely confident doing. We are the most guarded and private of personality types which can come across as cold or disinterested. Our personality makes it difficult to ask for help even if we need it. INTJ females have a strong Type A personality and the desire to take charge; we tend to thing no one can do something as well as we can. We struggle with making friends: our list of people to call if we need help is rather small. We don't bother keeping people around unless they are true friendships, not superficial. One of our largest weaknesses is the inability to make small talk in social situations (assuming we show up to the social situation to begin with). It takes a very special type of partner to see through our rough exterior and appreciate what we have to offer.

Wrapping Things Up

While it might seem a little overwhelming and lonely being the rarest female personality type, we INTJ women have many amazing traits that make us extraordinary. We don't open up to many people but once we have allowed someone into our inner circle, we are completely loyal. It's even more difficult to find a partner that can embrace and appreciate all of our quirks: once you've found that person it's likely long term, if not permanent, partnership. While it's great for us to have these relationships, we're also die-hard introverts that thrive on alone time. Others might wonder how we don't get lonely, but we are actually energized by solitude. After a long day of being around others, we need hours or even days to recover. It's not like these tendencies appeared out of thin air: we INTJ women were the young girls who didn't have many friends and spent the majority of our time nose-deep in a good book. Many people have no idea what to make of a woman with a bunch of stereotypical male traits: some people find us intimidating, mean, rude, or standoffish. People that think these things don't know us well; we are really very empathetic, loyal, and kind underneath the surface. Once others realize that while we don't want to participate in meaningless small talk, we're great people to have deep conversations or debates with if it's about a worthwhile topic.

At the end of the day, we are rare: it's possible none of us will bump into a fellow INTJ female in our daily lives. This also means others probably haven't bumped into one either and don't know how to handle us. We can't take this personally. There's nothing wrong with your personality and there's no reason to let others make you feel poorly because of it. Friends and partners that are worth having will value the complexities we INTJ women bring to the table. You're intelligent, introverted, factual: an INTJ female.

About the Expert

Caitlin Humbert is a head over heels wife, mom to several rescue animals, hiker, entrepreneur, and a passionate writer. She enjoys reading, camping, riding four wheelers, organizing and reorganizing everything. Caitlin has a Bachelor of Arts in Psychology from Northern Kentucky University where she studied various aspects of personality psychology: she is also part of the small subset of female INTJs. Having been an outcast the majority of her life due to her rare personality type, she chose to further investigate this small group of women who have mainly unpopular characteristics for a female and validate their traits and feelings.

HowExpert publishes quick 'how to' guides on all topics from A to Z by everyday experts. Visit HowExpert.com to learn more.

Recommended Resources

- HowExpert.com – Quick 'How To' Guides on All Topics from A to Z by Everyday Experts.
- HowExpert.com/free – Free HowExpert Email Newsletter.
- HowExpert.com/books – HowExpert Books
- HowExpert.com/courses – HowExpert Courses
- HowExpert.com/clothing – HowExpert Clothing
- HowExpert.com/membership – HowExpert Membership Site
- HowExpert.com/affiliates – HowExpert Affiliate Program
- HowExpert.com/writers – Write About Your #1 Passion/Knowledge/Expertise & Become a HowExpert Author.
- HowExpert.com/resources – Additional HowExpert Recommended Resources
- YouTube.com/HowExpert – Subscribe to HowExpert YouTube.
- Instagram.com/HowExpert – Follow HowExpert on Instagram.
- Facebook.com/HowExpert – Follow HowExpert on Facebook.

Printed in the USA
CPSIA information can be obtained
at www.ICGtesting.com
LVHW012259070824
787682LV00025B/813